EMPOWERED

The Woman's Guide to Following Your Heart

one woman's journey to her purpose

Jenny Powers

For my heart, that has always believed

EMPOWERED

The Woman's Guide to Following Your Heart

Introduction

A year ago, I set out to find my greatest purpose in life. I left a life that I knew very well, a very safe life with lots of predictability. I left it all to follow my heart. What has unfolded has been a journey that has led me to a mission, a mission that I believe in with every fiber of my being. The vision for this mission has many pieces and continues to unfold as I write this. However, the mission is the same.

To empower women everywhere to become our best selves. To awaken us to our own power so that we may live as the women that we are born to be. To free us from what we carry around as the caretakers of others so that we take the time to stop, breathe and reconnect to who we each are. To strengthen our relationship with ourselves so that we embrace our bodies, our hearts, our minds and our spirits, in everything we do. To build the tools that are necessary for us to be able to unleash the potential that is inside all of us so that we are each capable of doing amazing things. To grant us the space in this world where we can experience the freedom to feel, to express, to let it all out and to connect to our happiest selves. To honor and celebrate the brilliance, the passion, the fire and the joy of women, everywhere. To create the place on this Earth where extraordinary transformation happens so that we are all empowered to live our best lives.

When I began this journey, I began to write a blog. This book is inspired by that blog. It started as a way for me to inspire others, but it soon became a way for me to inspire myself. It became a way for me to track my own experiences, a way for me to understand all that I was feeling, a way for me to work through everything that I was going through and a way for me to chronicle my journey. It became the place where I expressed myself – fully, openly and honestly – and in doing so, came to find some peace along the way in leaning on what I learned through what I wrote. I am still on the journey, but the revelations that I have experienced along the way are in these pages. They are authentic. They are genuine. This is truly the step-by-step journey that I have been on – nothing forced, created or manufactured for any other purpose than to express all that I felt in my heart at the time, as I found my way. These were not written for any effect or even with this book in my mind, so you can trust the integrity of these discoveries. I never intended to share my journey in this way, but I understand now, that I am meant to. The journey when you follow your heart is hard, and in moments, it can overwhelm you to the point where you feel like you will never find your way. But you will, I promise. If you just keep going. You may feel crazy, lost, uncertain, and so alone at times. May this book always remind you that you never are.

Sometimes in my darkest hour, the things that I discovered in these pages, have been my only light. I share them from this place. They are reliable truths. You can depend on them. They will show you the way. Use them as a light, as a reason to keep going, as a reason to keep believing, as a reason to never give up on your journey, on your dreams, on your heart and on yourself. It is not easy to follow your heart, to seek a life of purpose, to remain true to the song that is in your heart, the song that quietly whispers to you, the song that you are meant to sing that the rest of the world has yet to hear. But you must. The world needs you. To live the life that you are meant to live and to become the woman that you are meant to become. You are here for a reason. We are each here for a purpose, a purpose that is uniquely our own. But the only way that we will each get to our purpose and live our best life, is if we each share the story of our journey and the guiding truths that we discover along the way. They are the light by which all of us will see.

These are my truths.

This is my journey.

Make This Your Beginning

I can make this the beginning of anything that I want. So I will. Here comes a vision so big that it will change the way that we as women feel about ourselves, about our bodies and about our power. It is going to be huge. We will own who we are again. We will stop apologizing for being as amazing as we are. We will spread our wings. And we will fly. Make today the beginning of anything that you want in your life. As soon as you do, it has begun.

Believe in the Magic

The world rewards courage with beauty. Growing pains are hard and giving birth to the song that is in my heart is testing my strength. Risking it all and putting my heart on the line is uncomfortable and the unknown of the journey can be overwhelming. I am living this. But the magic in this world understands this and recognizes my bravery and says, I see you and I am in awe of what you are willing to go through to give birth. The most beautiful complete double rainbow awaited me in the sky out my front door at the end of my first big day of following my heart. Believe in the magic.

Do What You Love

What do I love? I love inspiring women, including myself, to feel better about ourselves. This is what I love. This is where my joy is. Today was a huge step for me. I'm not sure how it will all unfold, but I do know that today, I walked the walk. I walked right through all of my fears, and did what I love to do in spite of them. I don't know exactly how life works, but I do know that amazing things must come from doing that. In your life, always do what you love. If you do, you will always love what you do.

Embrace These

Live Without Judgment

Open Your Mind

Believe the Best

Enjoy Nature

Laugh Freely

Love Deeply

Dance More

Hug Often

Feel Alive

Each of these makes my heart sing. They inspire me. They are what I choose to believe in. They are what I now live by. Embrace these in your life, especially the *Dance More*. They will bring you such joy.

Move Your Body

There are moments when I feel so unsure about what I am feeling. It is in these moments that I realize that I have allowed my body to sit idle for too long. I must always remember to move my body. The wisdom of my body is so much stronger than that of my mind. So when I want to unravel what I feel, when I want to understand the cluttered emotions that are running around in my head, I just move. Today, I did that. I shut off my mind and I moved my body. I stopped holding on, and I let all my emotions sink into my body. I let my body feel all that I was feeling and just began to move through it all. This puts the emotion into my body so that I don't have to think about it, so that I can feel it. This brings such clarity about what I feel. It connects me to the truth of my emotions. Every time. In the moments when you feel overwhelmed by all that you feel, simply move. Stretch your legs, lengthen your arms, allow your hands to reach for the sky. And breathe. Your body always knows the truth. You just have to let it speak, and listen.

Make Today That Day

I must recognize and enjoy the little victories of today. I must be present in the space in my life that is begging me to stop and say, today was enough. Today, I achieved enough, accomplished enough, did enough and made enough progress. If I don't stop today and say this and recognize my victories, then when will I? That day in the future will never come, if I don't make today that day. So I am making today that day. Today, revel in your little victories. Make today the day that was enough. Do this every "today" that follows because strung together, these todays are your life.

Shine Your Light

I must shine my light. I must unlock the power of the light that is inside of me and let it radiate for all to see. To my Get It Girl tribe of girls, you inspire me to do this every day. You have taught me what it is to own the power of my light and to let it shine, fully. With you, I stopped apologizing for my brilliance and I owned it. I shine my light now, always. Today, let the power of your light radiate from within you. Let your own light shine brightly and fully. You never know who you will inspire to shine their own light when you do.

Recognize Them

There are women in my life who quietly and unassumingly rest in the wings. They are women who seek little fanfare. They are women who remind me of my childlike joy with their passion for the simple things and add to my life with their heartfelt compassion. Recognize these women in your life. Spend time in their presence. They are the ones who always bring warmth to your heart.

Refuse to Conform

Today, I was walking and two rows of mailboxes stacked on top of each other caught my eye. Nine of the same boring standard black mailboxes labeled #1 through #9, and then one huge shiny white one in the top left corner labeled #49. Yes, #49 and white, for no apparent reason. I smiled because I knew immediately that that one white mailbox is me. Always marching to the beat of my own drum. Refusing to conform, refusing to fit in, refusing to fall in line with what others are doing or with what is expected of me. In your life, refuse to conform. Don't be like everyone else around you. In a crowd, only one stands out. Be that one.

Do the One Thing

What is the thing that scares me the most?

I know what it is. The first thing that popped into my head is the thing that I fear the most. It is also the thing that I must do, the most, to free myself from a block that is not real. I use fear as an excuse, as a reason to not do something, as justification for staying stuck, small and safe. Fear is not an actual thing that exists on this planet, but a figment of my imagination. If I was not afraid, I would dream bigger, risk more and live a life that is so full, rich and beautiful that fear would never again be a part of my life. So I will do the one thing. I will do the thing that scares me the most. Today, decide to do the one thing. Take one step towards the thing that first popped into your head, the perceived roadblock that you believe stands in the way of your greatest happiness, and realize that there is nothing to fear in doing it. There is just everything to gain. Your life is waiting for you on the other side of this step. Do the thing that scares you the most. Free yourself.

Celebrate Yourself

"Do something to celebrate yourself this weekend."

I just said this to a friend and as soon as I had said it, I realized that this is exactly what I need to do for myself. I need to take my own advice. It is hard to do as I continue to walk forward on this unknown path with what I have decided is very little to show for all my efforts. I am following my heart and yet I am the only one who continues to judge my efforts as not enough. I don't feel that I've earned the right to celebrate myself because I haven't done enough yet. In my own eyes, I haven't created something concrete or made enough tangible progress to warrant celebration and I am holding all that I have done up against standards so high that it is almost impossible to breathe. I am running myself ragged chasing the accomplishments, the achievements, the mile markers, and there is this quiet little voice inside of me that is desperately asking me to just stop. Breathe. Acknowledge all that you are and all that you have done and celebrate both. So I will do this. I will celebrate myself. Today, find the quiet little moments where there is nothing else to do but breathe and just allow yourself to celebrate all that you are. What you have created in your life, whatever that may be, and the person that you are, are extraordinary and you must stop judging either as anything less. And you must celebrate.

Live as You

"I'd rather die being myself than live trying to be someone else."

These words came out of my mouth today when I was talking to my sister and I then quoted myself about fourteen times throughout the rest of the day. There is nothing like being seriously and totally impressed with your own sheer brilliance. Because here's the thing, my epiphany today taught me that I honestly believe that living a life trying to be someone that I'm not, just so that other people will like me and approve of me and accept me, does actually seem worse to me than death. It's a life of unfulfilled potential, of diminished power, of unlived dreams, of giving up on myself - all of which leave me with a quiet desperation, a broken heart and a feeling of subdued suffering that somehow just never seems to end. To me, that has to be worse than death. So today I committed to this: I refuse to play by other people's rules, to dim my light so that others won't feel so threatened, to conform to others' standards and go quietly so that people won't be afraid of the ways that I might rock the boat or shake things up simply by being me and saying all I feel. I will not be someone else, or keep myself in a box, just so that others feel more comfortable and justified in staying in theirs. And if in doing this, it all ends for me, well at least I never gave up on me, at least I fought for what I believe in and stood my ground, against the odds. At least I lived as me. In your life, live only as you. It is the best person you will ever be.

Get Through the Beginning

"Don't give up, the beginning is always the hardest."

These words were just said to me by a friend, so I will trust that they are true. I will just keep going and get through my beginning. On your journey, just get through your beginning. The road that follows it is always easier.

Expect Exciting

In the moments when I expect something exciting to happen, it does. Always expect that something exciting is about to happen. Because it is.

Let Nobody Put You in a Corner

I am living equal parts *Dirty Dancing* and *Footloose*. I have created these dance classes as part of this mission to help all of us to embrace our bodies. But today, I was told that I had to take out the word "sexiest" in my class descriptions in order to be permitted use of a dance space. I almost died right there on the spot. This place had an image to uphold and well, sexiest just wasn't going to cut it. So I gave in, and played by their rules because genuinely, it was the only space that I had for that night. But inside I was left with this unsettling feeling of having been scolded, despite the fact that I didn't actually know what I had done wrong. And so later, when I told the story to a girlfriend, I genuinely used *Footloose* as a reference. I told her, if I could just find where it said "sexiest" in the Bible, I could go all Ren McCormack on this woman at the next town hall meeting and get them to let me use the old mill across the track and let me hold my classes. If I could find this word in the Bible, then, they would let me dance.

And now I find myself living out the *Dirty Dancing* part of this. For the past few weeks, I have been told by so many people to change the wording of my classes - use "exercise", take out "dance", add "fitness", really make people feel comfortable, like it's just working out and not a sexy dance class. Because apparently everyone on this planet is afraid of the word sexy. So I did, and I've tried that, and I've tried to live with that for the past few weeks. But here's the problem with that. My class is sexy and it is dance - and I am those things too. I am proud of the class that I have created and of all that it offers, and by making it a square peg so that it fits in the square hole that is this world, I have lost the beauty of all that it is. So, as Johnny Castle says in *Dirty Dancing* :

> *"Sorry about the disruption, folks, but I always do the last dance of the season. This year somebody told me not to. So I'm gonna do my kind of dancin' with a great partner, who's not only a terrific dancer, but somebody who's taught me that there are people willing to stand up for other people no matter what it costs them. Somebody who's taught me about the kind of person I want to be."*

Today, I stood up for the kind of woman that I want to be. I switched all of my marketing to be exactly what I want it to be, to describe the classes that I want to teach, to reflect the kind of dancing that I want to do. So, Baby, here's to you. Nobody puts me in a corner either. Let nobody put you in a corner. Ever. In anything you do. Walk up on that stage, and dance.

Surround Yourself

There are people in my life who can always feel the moments when I am just about to give in to challenges. And they arrive in exactly those moments to help get me through. A friend just did. Because she did, I didn't give in and I got through the challenge. We all need people to believe in us for when our belief in ourselves wavers. Remember to surround yourself with these people. They are so valuable. They are essential pieces of the bridge over which you will walk to your dreams. They are our soul mates. They are the people in our life who are connected to our journey. They are the people who always know the perfect moment to send exactly the inspiration that we need to keep going, to just keep believing. To my soul mates, you are a gift. I treasure you. In your life, surround yourself with your soul mates. Surround yourself with the people that believe in you. Build your bridge.

Stay Open

In my life, I cannot stay closed off. I cannot just keep deciding to play it safe. It is too uncomfortable. I am afraid to open, to uncover, to reveal, to express, to bare because opening up has hurt before. But any pain that I might feel in opening up again can't be greater than the ache that I feel now as I continue to play it safe, as I continue to protect myself. So I will take the chance, and I will open. I will let life in again. Today, decide to take the chance. Open to life. Though you may have been hurt in the past, you have one life. Live.

Be Crazy

I walked past an Apple store today and I was reminded of all the ways that they have changed our world. I have always loved their "Think Different" ad campaign, where they describe the people that are crazy being the ones who change the world. I have always felt that it was written just for me. I am crazy. I know this. Crazy enough to think that I can change the world. But because I am, I will. Be crazy. Crazy enough to think that you can do anything, achieve anything, believe anything, build anything, conceive of anything and dream up anything in this world. Because you are, you will.

Carve Your Own Path

On days like today, following the crowd feels so much easier to me. Because there is a level of certainty in the crowd and in the numbers of people that surround me. In a crowd, I am never alone. But when I walk in a crowd, I am never the first to discover anything new. I am never the first to discover something unique. I am never the first to discover something that I can call all my own. There is such passion to be found in discovering my own. So I will leave the crowd and I will set out on my own. And I will continue to carve the path in front of me, for as long as it takes for me to get to my own. When confronted with the choice, decide to leave the crowd. Set out on your own. Carve your own path through this world. It is how you will find the gold in undiscovered lands.

Get to Peace

I walked past a picture of Amelia Earhart today and was reminded of the value of courage. She believed that the way to be granted peace in your life was to always be willing to pay for it with your courage. Fearless women and their journeys continue to inspire me. Peace is what I want most in my life. Peace to me is knowing in my heart that I am where I am meant to be. Acting with courage is what the journey requires for me to have this peace. So I will keep choosing courage, and not fear, so that I may get to this peace. When given the choice between courage and fear, choose courage. It will take you to peace.

Endure Rejection

Growing, creating, stretching myself to limits that feel as uncomfortable as anything I have ever known is hard. It is torturous at times, because it requires that I experience rejection. And rejection is so painful. But I still believe that all of the emotion that comes with going for it, with risking it all, with seeking the big dream is still somehow better than all I will feel, or the complete nothingness and lack of any emotion, that will accompany my decision to do nothing, to just sit there and let the dream remain inside of me, untouched. This journey is testing my resolve. It is testing my capacity to keep going. It is testing my ability to weather the storm because it requires that I endure so much rejection along the way. But I will endure it, and I will keep going. Though it isn't easy to do, endure the rejection that comes on your journey, just get through it. But keep jumping off those cliffs. Because the pain that you will feel with rejection, the pain that you will feel if you fall, will always be less than the pain that you will feel if you never jump.

Do That One Thing, Seriously

Today, I did the thing that scared me most. I wrote about this before and about how the thing that I fear the most is also the thing that I need to do the most, the thing that I need to do more than anything else. Today, I did that thing. I practiced what I preached. To me, that is everything that this mission stands for. Inspiring others by leading, by being the one that is willing to go first, by risking doing the things that might be scary in hopes of shining more light on the darkness that is hiding our collective brilliance. By taking steps towards what I want and refusing to be held back by what I fear. My mind and inner critic want to just judge the results, to overlook my action of simply doing this thing. But my heart recognizes the value of the action and my courage so I am living in just honoring those. Refusing to be held back by fear and pushing the limits of what I believe I'm capable of is everything. It gives me wings and allows me to soar into the life that I want to live. So today, take the leap. Refuse to be held back by what you fear and do the thing that scares you most. You will be astounded at how free you feel when you do.

Believe That You Can

Today, I will believe that I can. Because I do, I will be able to do anything that I set my mind to. No one else gets to decide what I am going to believe. It is always up to me. There are no rules that I have to follow about what I can and can't believe. I am always free to choose. You create your own reality by what you decide to believe you can do. Decide to believe that you can, and you will.

Welcome Them In

At a certain point, it stops being about where you're going and starts being about where you are.

This was the thought that popped into my head last night, and it resonated so deeply. I feel like I have been chasing a dream my whole life, chasing a future that feels so bright and a purpose that feels like it could fill the entire universe. It has been an exhausting search, the pressure of fulfilling my destiny often sucking all of the air out of any room for me. I want to fulfill it, believe me, it has driven me my whole life, but there is something in me that is shifting, softening, opening up to the fact that chasing this enormous future is making my life an incredibly trying journey. So I started thinking. What are the experiences that I keep envisioning in this future, that I see in this big life that awaits me, that I still want to have? What do I want to do that I haven't done yet? It made me put the brakes on. It made me stop and say, if my time was limited, what would I still want to experience in my life?

I have begun a list and I have opened my heart to welcoming these experiences into my life. Because I am tired of waiting for my future to begin so that I can finally have these experiences that I want. I am ready for them and I want them to fill my days. Now. I am afraid that they won't be enough, that they won't live up to all that I have envisioned them to be in my imaginary future for so long. But here's the thing with that, this imaginary future is wearing me out. It doesn't feel like anything, except a whole lot of focused thinking and pressure to hurry up and get there, soon, so I can begin. So I will unlock and open the door. I will throw out the welcome mat to these experiences that I want to have because they aren't getting any closer to me by keeping them safely nestled in my future. I will welcome them to be a part of my today. There are experiences in your life that you want to have. When they arrive, just say yes to them. Welcome them in. You are ready for them now. Make your future start today.

Discover Your Destiny

I love to let my mind wander, to let it roam, to let it run freely throughout the corners of my imagination without telling it where to go. When I do this, I love to see where it takes me. It always reveals something to me about where I truly want to go and what I truly want to do. I did this today and found myself somewhere unexpected. When you close your eyes, and allow your mind to dream, to wander, to go exactly where it wants to go with no limitations, where are you? This is where you are meant to be and it is what you are meant to do. It is your destiny. So today, close your eyes and just allow your mind to wander. See where it leads you. Welcome to your destiny.

Trust Yourself

In the moments when I doubt myself, I must always remember that I know so much more than I think that I do. I can trust myself. I am empowered by my experience, by my strength, by my resilience, and by my wisdom, all of which have come from my journey. You are too. Your experiences have made you a very wise woman. Trust yourself.

Value Your Presence

I must always remember that my presence matters. I must remember that even after I have left a room, my presence lingers and affects the lives of those I come into contact with. I think that people forget me, or don't think about me when I am not with them, because I never see how my presence affects them in these moments. So I never know how what I experience with them might shift something in their life, or make them feel something that affects them deeply. So I must always remember to value my presence. Never underestimate your influence in this world. A simple thing, a quiet moment that you might never think twice about could shift the way that another person sees the world and lives their life. Value the power that your presence holds. Treat yourself and your place in this world with the utmost respect. Because you never know whose life you touch while you're not watching.

Have Big Dreams

To have big dreams is a matter of choice. To then reach those dreams becomes a matter of discipline. I have big dreams. People even laugh when I describe them. I have no idea how my dreams are going to happen. That scares me. The size of my dreams scares me too. They are enormous. But if I just keep going, and live with the discipline that they require, then no one can stop me from making them come true. You always get to choose the size of your dreams. So have big dreams. If you live with the discipline that is required to get there, you will watch them come true.

<u>Dive</u>

I never seem to be content just living in the shallow waters of my life. I always find myself diving deeper, searching for the greater meaning, exploring the unknown waters that sit below the glimmer of the superficial surface. Don't settle for living a shallow life. Seek deeper meaning, in everything that you do. Explore the depths. They are where the treasure chest is always found.

Let Them Rise Up

I am listening deeply, openly, and passionately to the voices in me that are rising up as I grow into the woman that I am meant to become. Some are voices connected to pieces of me that I have long since lost touch with and must reclaim. Some are voices connected to new pieces of me that are finally finding their footing and are just being born. When these voices speak, I must let them be heard. When the quiet little voices that have been inside of you begin to speak loudly, you must listen. Whether they speak to a piece of you that you must reconnect to or a new piece of you that has finally emerged, you must allow these voices to rise up. You must let them be heard. They will bring you such wisdom.

Pursue What You Want Most

I can't give up what I want most in life, for what I want right now. So I will keep going, for what I want most. To live my greatest purpose. There are so many things that I want now, that I have had to give up temporarily as I find this purpose – an income, a stable job, a home and space of my own, relationships and romantic connections, my social life and the adventures I had, time with my friends – and in moments, this has broken my heart. Because these things are so important to me. They give my life such balance. But they are not what I want most. What I want most is to live my greatest purpose. So I will keep going until I have what I want most, and trust that all those things that I want now, every single one of them, will be there when I do. Pursue what you want most in your life, whatever that may be for you. Because when you have what you want most, everything else will have such meaning.

Grow Where You Are

I must trust where I am, even though it isn't easy for me to do this. So much about where I am right now doesn't seem right for me and feels hard. But in my heart, I know that this is where I have to be. I know that this is where I have to grow. So I will grow here. Though it may seem wrong or not where you want to be or wish you were, you are where you are in your life for a reason. It is in this place that you are planting seeds that are essential. They are the seeds that will enable you to live your best life. Sometimes, it is uncomfortable to be where your heart has led you. But seeds must be planted there. Weather the discomfort and grow where you are.

Take One Step at a Time

I will get to where I am trying to go if I just allow the plan for my journey to take me there. But so often I get in a rush and I want to just get there. Now. But there are steps in my journey and each one of them is always leading me closer to where I want to go. I put so much pressure on myself, thinking that I am supposed to know the whole plan, now. I panic when I don't. But I'm not supposed to know the whole plan. I can't. I never could, or else I would never get out of bed in the morning because there would be too much information for me to process. So the steps in my journey are there to protect me and the way that they unfold one at a time keeps me from being overwhelmed by having to process my entire journey at once. When you feel overwhelmed by your journey and feel the pressure to know more of the plan than you do, just relax. The steps in your journey will guide you. Take one step at a time and know that you will get to where you are trying to go. The steps will take you there.

Just Be

Sometimes, I can get so focused on doing that I forget to just be. But there is such value in just being. When I stop doing and I allow myself to be, I feel. There is such wisdom available in this silence. The silence of just being is always waiting to guide you. Connect to this wisdom. Just be.

Realize You Will Be Led

In moments like this, when all the light has gone in my life, and darkness surrounds me, it is hard to believe that the light will return. But it always does. This inspires me now. Darkness is hard to get through, but one way or another, the light always arrives to guide me out of it. So even in your darkest moments, when all the light has gone, you must always believe that it will return. In the moments when you can't see in front of you, always believe that the light will return to show you the way. Realize you will be led out of the darkness. Because every time, you are.

Honor All Love

I honor all love. I do because love heals. Decide to honor all love in this world. Because love on this Earth, is everything.

Get Back Up

So often, I think that I am the only one that has ever failed. Because I am the only one that I ever see fail. But I'm not. I think that those that I deem successful have never failed because I never see them fail. In a society where we can glamorize and highlight all that is good, I think that that is all that exists because that is all that we choose to discuss. Those who are well-known and whose lives we choose to follow rarely talk about their bad days, and those that we know more personally rarely turn to social media to discuss a day where they feel that they have failed miserably or a day where they felt less than adequate, in any way. We see the successes, and as a society, we tend to hide the failures, so we internalize that they don't exist for others. We then believe that we are the only one that has ever failed because our own failures are the only ones that we know. So I honor the courage of those of us that are willing to discuss our failures. They exist for everyone. And those of us that are willing to endure them, to survive them, to pick ourselves up and get back up again are the ones who succeed. Life is not without failure. But it is without success if you allow your failures to define you. Define yourself instead by your willingness to never give up, to never settle and get back up. If you do, success awaits you.

Try to Let Go

I am working through this everyday. It is hard to do. I want to control everything, in every way. And I am afraid to let go. Yet the key to my life is in the letting go. It is in the giving up of my need to always direct it, to steer it and to make it what I want it to be. Because trying to do this is exhausting me and it isn't working. So I must trust that the easiest, happiest, most fulfilling life, the life that I want to live, will only show up if I am willing to let go of my need to control everything. I am not there yet. But I want to be. I want to stop draining my power by running around trying to keep every ball in the air, always. I want to open my heart and my life to letting go because my need to control everything is stealing my peace of mind. So I will let go. I don't know how to do that exactly or if I can, but I will try. Today, try to let go of things, just for a bit. Try to relinquish the firm grip that you have on the need to control everything, even if it is just for a moment. Because maybe, if you let one ball drop, and the world doesn't end, you just might find some peace of mind.

Engage the Power

Sometimes, my mind sets barriers to what I believe I can do. But every time it does, my heart goes and breaks through each one of them. If my mind tells me that I can't do something, my heart goes and proves it wrong. Every single time. My mind is strong, but my heart is stronger. Engage the power of your heart and use it to break through walls. They will come crashing down every time.

Be Gentle with Yourself

This is tough for me to do. In the moments like now when things go wrong, I am so much better at being hard on myself. But this never makes me feel better, ever. So here's to replacing the harsh eyes through which I look at myself with gentle ones. Be gentle with yourself. See yourself through the compassionate eyes that you would use to look at someone else. Handle yourself like the precious jewel that you are.

Be Grateful for What You Have

The things in my life that I take for granted are the things that someone else is praying for. Accidents happen. I cut my hand cleaning a knife. It has rendered me virtually incapable of using my right hand for a while. I am right-handed, which means that everything is that much harder. In a moment, things can change. I am so aware of this right now and the things that I take for granted other people might be praying for. The ease of my body. The intricate and brilliant behind-the-scenes workings of my body that I am rarely aware of, that quietly and reliably function every day without my conscious effort. So, I am taking the time to see that these small things that I might have overlooked are the big things. Without a healthy body, I am incapable of living my best life. I am living in complete gratitude of my amazing body and all that it is capable of and I am appreciating every inch of it. Today, see the little things, and see the big things, too. And be grateful for all of them. Be grateful for everything that you do have. Because to someone else, just one of those things, might be everything.

Enjoy Your Curves

As a woman, I must be inspired by my feminine grace and enjoy my beautiful curves. I must remember the power that they hold, and stop apologizing for them or feel the pressure to make them different. May we usher in the return to an era where we as women are celebrated and revered for the power that our bodies hold, not condemned, criticized and judged by their shape or size. May we usher in a new era, where we as women are encouraged to take up more space in this world, to honor our bodies, to own our breasts and our hips, just as they are, so that we may then be able to channel our energy into being healthier, happier and stronger. May it only be about how we feel to ourselves that defines the health of our body, not about how we look to others. May we always empower each other to feel good about the unique shape of each of our bodies. Your body is a temple. And you have the permission to treat it as such, in the unique shape that you are. So today, walk more proudly and more confidently than you ever have. Own your power. Enjoy your beautiful curves.

Appreciate All of Your Beauty

My own beauty is maximized when I am the best possible version of myself on the inside and on the outside. But I can lose sight of this. So often, I find myself valuing just the outside in feeling my beauty and I overlook the fact that my beauty is just as much about what is on the inside of me. It sounds obvious that I shouldn't do this, but sometimes, I still do. I am always working to become the best version of myself on the inside and on the outside. Not the most beautiful version according to someone else's standards, but the best version according to my own. Remember to always appreciate who you are becoming on the inside and on the outside when embracing your own beauty. Together, they are all of you.

Choose New

I want to experience new things. But often I find such comfort in routine, in treading the same path, in living as a creature of habit safely nestled in my familiar surroundings. Yet I still want to experience new things. However, I realize now in looking at my patterns, that I can't create the life that I want with these new experiences, without actually doing these new things. Though wishing, hoping and praying them into existence seems so much easier, it doesn't work. I must actually do these things in order for them to be real. Sometimes new is scary, but experiencing new things will not happen if I decide to stay on the well-worn path of routine. So I will step into new. In your life, shed your identity as a creature of habit. Shake things up. Choose new.

Believe in Abundance

I do now. Abundance is what I now believe in, in everything. I never have before, so this is new for me. But I am going to, because it is what I want to experience. Decide to believe in abundance, in every area of your life. And watch it arrive.

Live in Possible

My dreams feel impossible right now. And yet something in me is still going. Something in me must believe that they are possible. I look forward to the day very soon when the part of me that believes they are possible can sit back and finally say to the rest of me, "See, I was right. It was all possible." Everything is possible. Things always seem impossible, to everyone who has created something great. But everything is possible. Live with the understanding that it is.

Recognize the Diamonds

I have done so much work on my life and on myself. I have risked everything and have had the courage to go into the darkness inside of me. And because I have, I now sparkle with a clarity that is bright because I have done the work to remove anything blocking the brilliance of my light. Today, I take pride in my journey, in having done the work, in the clarity of the light that comes from within me, because it did not just come to exist on its own. I recognize my struggle and honor all that it has taken for me to get here. I own the brilliance of the light that emanates from within me, because I have done the work on my life and on myself that allows it to radiate. Recognize the people in your life that have done the work. Recognize the people who sparkle from within. They are diamonds that have been shaped by life.

Cherish Your Body

I must always remember to embrace and cherish my body because it is the most amazing thing that I will ever own. We can all lose sight of this so easily and spend moments blaming our bodies for not being exactly what we want them to be or not doing exactly what we want them to do. We can put our focus on what they are not, rather than all that they are and all that they do for us every single day. We must remember to cherish them, to honor them and to take care of them. We must nourish them with good food and keep them healthy with exercise. Though sometimes both can feel like such work, we must see these as ways that we celebrate our bodies and honor their capability. If we can view food and exercise in this way, and not as things to get through or a way for us to blame and punish ourselves for everything that we think we're not, then both become fun again. Food that nourishes our body should be enjoyed. It feels good. And exercise is how we take care of our bodies and our minds and should connect us to the strength of both, not highlight the places that we think we fall short. It should make us feel better and inspire and uplift us, not discourage us because we are nowhere near the impossible standards that we keep trying to meet. Good food and exercise are how we show appreciation for our bodies, for their wonder. Choose them. Go for a walk, try a class, get a friend and go stroll through the woods. And the next time that you do, just simply focus on feeling the wonder of your body and all that it is capable of. Just let that be enough and get rid of all other expectations. Your body is a gift. It is the best one that you will ever get. Cherish it.

Love Your Sisters

Sisters make such amazing friends. They are so special. They make life that much more fun. My sister is extraordinary and her love and support of me lifts me up and gives me wings in the moments when flying feels all but impossible to me. Our sisterhood was given to us. Our friendship has been created by us as a choice through the years. I honor the amazing woman that she is and recognize the unbelievable gift that we share in the friendship that we have built together. Whether they are your sisters by birth or not, you know who they are. Love them. That bond is priceless.

Stand in the Sunshine

It is so simple. Sometimes, there is nothing on this Earth that feels better than standing in the sunshine. So today, I will just linger a little bit longer. Stand in the sunshine today and allow its rays to dance across your skin. Embrace its warmth. Because the sun is there, shining, waiting just to celebrate you.

Leave Your Legacy

I was in a bookstore today and walked past a book entitled *Well-Behaved Women Seldom Make History.* And it made me realize, they don't. So I will refuse to behave. I will refuse to obey. I will refuse to play small. I will refuse to be held back. I will refuse to give up. I will refuse to play by the rules that other people tell me to follow. I will refuse to listen to or to see any limitations in this world. I will refuse to stop talking. I will refuse to go quietly. I will refuse to sit down. In anything you do, cause a stir. Make waves. Ruffle feathers. Passionately stand up for everything that you believe in. This is how you make history. This is how you leave your legacy.

Be a Leader

Today, I am inspired to lead. I am inspired to pave the way.
Being a leader means going first. It means walking ahead. It
means knowing the power of your influence, and using it to
open the doors through which others will walk to their dreams.
I am a leader and I own my influence. Be one too. Go first.
Lead.

Survive the Rain

Today, the rains in my life fell so hard that I could barely breathe. The pain of frustration on this journey, the fear of the unknown, the challenge of not being able to figure out how to live the life that I want to live and do all the things that I want to do hit me hard. But I let the tears fall and I weathered the storm. Some days, it is just about surviving the rain. Today, it was for me and I did. When the rains in your life come, just let them fall. Survive them. Your rainbow is coming.

Decide Who You Are

Dear Me,

You are the sexiest thing that has ever walked the face of this Earth.

Love, Me

This is who I have decided I want to be. So this is who I am. It is the relationship that I aspire to have with myself, always. To say what I am and own it, without needing anyone else to validate what I believe I am or to define me. I can know who I am and decide who I want to be without needing anyone else to tell me or to approve of it. That is owning my truth and not apologizing for a single brilliant thing that I decide to be. You too can be anything that you want to be. So decide who you want to be. The moment you do, that is who you are.

Forgive Yourself

This is my lesson for today. I need to learn to forgive myself for my mistakes. It feels impossible sometimes, but I must. And I have to learn to take pride in my mistakes, because my mistakes mean that I'm trying. The only true failure in life is not trying, so if I am going to truly live, I have to try. And if I am going to try, then I am going to make mistakes. They are inevitable, for everyone who is succeeding.

But they are so hard to go through. I spend so much time punishing and blaming myself for decisions that I made that didn't turn out so well, despite the fact that deep down, I know that doing this doesn't actually change anything. It only robs me of the present and makes me feel terrible, and endlessly making myself feel guilty and culpable for what I think I should have known or wish I had at the time, doesn't ever help me. Ever. Mistakes are how we learn valuable lessons, and we can only learn the lesson by going through the experience, by making the mistake. Though I wish there were, there is no other way. Every experience, good or bad, happens for a reason, and there is a lesson in every single one of them. If we can take the lesson, then every single experience becomes valuable. Not easy to go through, but valuable. Because we are then empowered with the knowledge that we gain from them, and once we have this knowledge, we are able to make a different decision the next time around. If we can view our life from this perspective, then forgiveness of ourselves and compassion for our journey are there.

When you are following your heart, when you are trying, the lessons will be there, but they are there to support you, not to punish you. They are there to guide you, to shape you, to help you. So embrace them and forgive yourself. Be grateful for what you now know and use this knowledge as a reason to make peace with the experiences. It is time to move on. Your life is desperately waiting for you to stop beating yourself up, and to reclaim your rightful place in the world. It is where you belong.

Live the Width

This is how I am building my life. I want to experience the width of my life and not just the length. I want to experience every single thing that I can while I am here on this Earth. It is what drives me and constantly fuels everything I do. You live the width of your life by saying yes to every experience that intrigues you along the way. Live the width of your life. It is what gives the length meaning.

Remember to Smile

Sometimes, I am way too busy taking life far too seriously for my own good, and I forget to smile. But I can never underestimate the power of a smile. It can change my day. And it can change someone else's day too. Because when I smile, I am immediately reminded of the things that are worth smiling about and I feel my own joy. And others around me are affected by my joy too. So in your life, always remember to smile. There is always something to smile about. Some days, it is harder to find, but keep looking because there always is. And when you find it, just smile. Feel your own joy radiate from within you. Then watch as the world around you is changed by your smile. You will make it glow.

Love Yourself First

I can lose myself so easily. To get myself back, I must love myself first. That is the only way that I fill my well from which I can once again give to my own life and to others. I am not used to loving myself first, because I am engrained to think that there is greater value in loving others before I love myself, but I must learn. Others can come next, but I must come first. To do this, I must truly acknowledge and value my own needs and desires. And I must do whatever it takes to get those needs and desires met. In your life, you must love yourself first. It might be new and feel hard to do, but you must try. For this moment, love yourself first. Let go of the guilt, own what you need and take steps toward getting those needs met. Fill your well. When you do, you will realize that everyone else in your life gets the best you when you love yourself first.

Say You Are Enough

Some days, I have to stop and say, "I am enough".   Today, I am saying this. I am enough. Stop right now, and say this too. You are enough. Own that it's true.

Paint Your Color

I love pink. I must paint with pink in the things that I do. We each love a different color. We each must paint with this color. If you love pink, then love pink, be pink, live pink, paint pink. If you love blue, paint blue. Paint in your life with the color of the rainbow that you love. A rainbow needs every color in it in order for it to be able to exist and the most beautiful rainbows are the ones that are the most colorful. Only you can be fabulous, wonderful, perfectly colorful you. Leave your mark in everything that you do. Paint your vibrant color across the sky. Decorate the world.

Be Present

In my life, I must be present every day. Today, I feel myself trying to be in the future, or at least think my way into it, and I am overlooking all that today is. The present is the only place that my life is ever real, and if I spend my time looking towards the future or dwelling on the past, I miss the experience of today. So I must live just my today. Look around you. Be present in your life, and see your today. It is so full of brilliance.

Take a Break

Sometimes I feel like I am holding on for dear life. And I'm afraid to take a break because the vision, the inspiration, the idea will go away. Because I think that nothing happens in a break. But so much actually does. Breaks are how I restore. They are how I rejuvenate. Without them, I just burn out. I am not good at taking them. But I must learn. This journey requires strength, determination and sheer will, all of which require energy. Taking a break is the only way that I can recharge my battery, restore this energy and be able to step back and reflect on how far I have come. I must take a break. In your life, you'll know when you need one, and when you do, you must honor this voice. You must take a break. When you do, put everything away, turn off your phone, shut down your computer. Stop and put your feet up. Seriously, phone off. Feet up. Now look back over your shoulder. See where you started and acknowledge just how far you have come. You must recognize all that you have done because it is really amazing. Be astonished at your progress. Yes, astonished. There is always huge progress and you must see it. Commit to taking breaks. And when you do, put your feet up, take a deep breath and look back over your shoulder. It is an astonishing view.

Feel Pleasure

My life is supposed to feel good. I am here to experience life and life is about pleasure. I am not here to spend my energy denying myself it. So I must remember to let myself feel pleasure. We can waste so much time keeping our bodies, our hearts, our minds and our spirits from enjoying pleasure. But when we do, we are getting it wrong. Pleasure is our birthright. We are each entitled to experience as much of it as we would like to experience in our life. So if it feels good, do it. If it brings you pleasure, do it. Seek to experience as much pleasure as you possibly can in your life, in everything you do. This will make your life fun. And you are here to have fun. Today, and every day, let yourself feel pleasure. Let your life feel so good.

Speak the Truth

I must speak my truth, always. As women, we are often so busy trying to meet expectations that we fail to honor our own feelings. But our feelings are right and justified. We are entitled to feel each and every one of them and we are allowed to tell people how we feel. This is the only way that we build a truly authentic and empowered life. This is the only way that we build a life that feels good to us. In every moment, speak your truth. And never stop.

Prioritize Smart

Smart is the new sexy. It is actually, the real sexy. Smart is the sexiest thing I can be. Smart is my number one priority. Make it yours too. Don't chase the ideal body type, the perfect wardrobe, the fabulous pair of shoes or the man that is going to save you. Be the master of your own destiny. Your intelligence will get you everything. Own its capability and do everything that you can to maximize, benefit from and utilize its power. It is the sexiest thing you will ever do.

March Yourself to Yes

I am working through an extraordinary number of no's right now in my life. And I am trying to find a way to make my peace with all of them. They are heartbreaking and are hard to experience. I want help with this whole vision, so these no's hurt, a lot. But every time they happen, I have to rely on my own talents to get things done. I am forced to dig inside of myself to march myself to the yes's. This is demanding and it is so much work, but I can see that there is such value in this. Because with every no, my confidence in my own abilities grows stronger and I am reminded of how truly capable I am. And right now, I do it best. It is my vision, my passion, my heart and no one else is willing to fight for it like I am. So I will embrace these no's and keep marching towards the yes's. The right plan, the right opportunities and the right support are waiting for me behind all the doors marked yes. May I arrive at them soon. May they open wide for me to enter. In your life, when no comes, embrace it. Dig inside of yourself. Realize how capable you truly are. And march yourself to yes.

Keep Swimming

A friend, inspired by *Finding Nemo* and seeing my struggle, told me today to just keep swimming. It is my inspiration for my day. I will just keep swimming. Some days, this feels like all you can manage. But on the days when it does, just keep swimming. Every time you do, it is enough.

Understand You Are Unstoppable

There is nothing on this Earth that can stop me from living exactly the life that I want to live and from having everything that I want to have. It is just not possible. There is nothing that can stop you either. Nothing. You are unstoppable.

Fight Through Hell

In the moments when nothing in my life seems to make sense, inspiration always comes in the most unexpected form. I was walking out of a supermarket today and a greeting card with wisdom from Winston Churchill caught my eye. His words, which read "if you're going through hell, keep going", arrived in the moment that I needed them most. Because I am going through hell. So I will just keep going. In your life, when you feel like you're going through hell, just keep fighting. Heaven awaits.

Characterize Yourself by the Moments After

It is in moments like these that I have found out who I am. I have often defined myself by the changes and by the challenges - by the failure, by the stumbling, by the mistakes that I've made that I wished I hadn't. But this is not what matters. What matters is what came next. Did I learn, did I grow, did I evolve, did I change, did the woman that I became do it differently the next time around? In every instance, like now, I have. That is extraordinary. These challenges, both epic and small, have made me who I am. This is a woman that I fall more and more in love with every day. Look at the times in your life when you've stumbled. Then look at the moments that came after. Define yourself by these moments after. They are who you are.

Define Your Success

Did I live my purpose?

Success to me is living my purpose. It is the only success that I care to achieve. It takes a lot of courage to live with this definition, because society can make it all about fame, money and the accumulation of things. Society can define success by material wealth and use it as the benchmark to define the level of your success as a person and of your life. But it is not about these things to me because none of these things speak to the actual value of a life. Did you make the world a happier place, did you change the lives of people that you met for the better, did you add sunshine, love, laughter, and joy to the world and inspire those that you met? Did you make people smile and laugh, and make them feel better as a result of having been in your presence? This is what matters. Look at your success in the way that you touch lives, in the way that you uplift those that you are around, in the way that you encourage those that you meet to reach for the stars and to believe in themselves and in their dreams. If I live out my greatest purpose on this Earth, and embody the woman that I am meant to be to the fullest extent that I am capable of, and spread as much love, joy and happiness as I possibly can, and create as much positive change in the world as I can, then I will have lived the most successful life that I can live. That is what success is to me. So define your own success based on what is important to you and based on what success means to you. Then live your life using only that definition.

Pick the Worthwhile Way

Sustaining a belief in positively transforming the world is exhausting. I am living this every day. But now that the light has been shone on this desire, I can never again live in the darkness that I used to know, where I didn't feel connected to this vision and feel how capable I am. That darkness is gone. I have glimpsed a bigger vision and now that I have seen it, there is no going back to a time when I hadn't seen it. That vision is here, so there is now no other worthwhile way for me to go. It might cost me everything, but I will have to find a way to sustain this belief. Once you have seen this vision, once you know that you are capable of making the world a better place, there becomes only one worthwhile way to go. Pick that way. Transform the world.

Commit to Great Work

We can get so focused on the jobs, the titles and the salaries that we can lose sight of what truly matters in all of these. The actual work that we're doing, the difference that we're making. These are what matter. I am here to do great work. It is the work I commit to doing in my life. Great work is the work that matters to me. It is the work that brings joy to my heart. It is the work that feels important, to me. Sometimes in life, you don't always know what the job or position might look like that will allow you to do great work, but you always know what great work feels like when you're doing it. You are entitled to do it. Commit to doing great work in your life. Commit to the work that feels great.

Value Your Growth

Some days, it is hard to keep following my heart, because my heart is leading me to experiences that hurt, that challenge me, that knock me down. The way of my heart sometimes feels harder, because it is on this path that I am forced to grow. But growth is the key. It is work to live through it, a lot of work, and the pain of growth can feel unbearable at times because the process is breaking me apart. My growth challenges me and sometimes involves pain, suffering and heartbreak because in it, I am forced to let go of everything that I've been. I am forced to let go of who I have been so that I may become the woman that I am meant to be. But as I do, extraordinary things happen. The real me begins to emerge, and can shine and breathe and thrive and soar. So keep following your heart, despite any struggles that it may take you to. It is guiding you to these difficult experiences to help you. It is guiding you to the experiences that will help you to grow so that you may become the woman that you are meant to become. Value your growth. Know that your heart will always lead you through it.

Trust Great Pains

From great pain comes great triumph. I believe this. It is taking everything in me to keep going because I feel such pain in trying to give birth to this vision. But I will believe that from the greatest pains come the greatest triumphs. So I will trust the magnitude of all that I feel and believe that it will result in the arrival of my greatest triumphs. As you follow your heart, trust the size of the pain that you might feel on your journey. It means that greatness is coming.

Believe We Are Connected

This is what I believe - that we are all just one piece of a beautiful puzzle. To me, there is such beauty in this belief. Sometimes we get so focused on the separate lives that we each lead. But we must believe that our lives are connected. We must believe that the decisions that we make are part of a much bigger plan and that they affect the lives of those with whom we share this world. If we believe this, if we believe that we are all part of the same masterpiece, it will unite us.

Unlock Your Potential

I want to know what lies inside of me. I don't understand what it is yet, but I know that it is the most extraordinary thing that I will ever know. It is my greatest potential. It is all that I am capable of. I want to unlock it, to connect to the wisdom that lives in me, to let it be the only thing that guides me in everything I do. Nothing or anyone outside of me is ever the source of my potential. It is always inside of me. So unlocking my potential is always within my control. Your potential is within your control too. All that you are capable of is always inside of you. So look inside of yourself, see everything that you are capable of being and decide to let it all out. Unlock your potential. Feel the power that comes from being all of you.

Choose to be Happy

This is the work for me now. I am having a hard time with this. My life isn't what I want it to be yet and I don't have all that I want. But I want to be happy. Now. I don't want to wait for happiness. So I will choose to be happy now, with everything that I have and with exactly where I am. I am happy, right here and right now, because I decided to be. Happiness is a decision that you make. It is not something that you wait on. Choose to be happy. The moment you do, you are.

Use Your Imagination

In my imagination, I can see the life that I want so clearly. This means that it can exist. This means that it can be real. The things that I imagine in this life that I want have all come from things that exist in this world. My dream life has been built from things that I have seen which means that it can be real. This means that I can have this life. Use your imagination as the canvas upon which you paint your dream life. There is so much power in doing this. Because once you can see it, you can have it.

Be Open to Change

Change is never easy. In it, we fight to hold on and we fight to let go. I am fighting to hold on. I am fighting to let go. I am just fighting, everything. When you are in the midst of change, it is impossible to escape it. It is everywhere. But since it is everywhere, it must be changing so much. So I will keep breathing and keep fighting through it. The reality of the life that I want is coming. I can feel it. All of this change is preparing me, to be able to thrive, succeed and soar in that reality. I know that. I am being prepared for my best life and in order to be able to live it, I must be my best self. I can only get there through this change. In order to be able to authentically stand behind this mission, I have to have gone through all the changes so that I know what this journey entails. I have to know what every step demands. I have to have done all the work in becoming my own best self so that I know what the journey requires. This is how empathy, compassion and understanding will be born. In order to truly empower women in the way that I want to, I have to have gone first. I must first have lived this mission, so that I am able to look every woman in the eye and say, yes, I know. This is the only way that true connection, true inspiration and true change will happen. So I will keep fighting through this change, no matter how painful it is, so that I know. All of it. Be open to the big change in your life. And when it arrives, trust it. It means that you are on your way to becoming the woman that you were born to be. And it means that you're close.

Move Mountains

I have been given the talents that I have in my life for a reason. It is my job to use them to do everything that I can do, to do everything that I was born to do. Many of these things are hard to do, but I am capable of doing them, so I must. And I will stop at nothing until I do. Never settle for doing anything less than you are capable of doing with the talents that you have. You have been given these talents for a reason. To move mountains.

Take Action

My dreams won't happen without action. Thinking is important. But too much thinking stops me dead in my tracks. The only way that I can get going again is by taking action. If you get stuck in your head, take action. It doesn't matter how big or small, just do something. Anything. Dreams happen when you do.

See No Limits

There are no limits to what I can do, not a single one. I feel this. But the only way that I will truly know it, is if I push myself to any limits that I think exist for me and then push myself right through all of them. So I will do this. You have unlimited capabilities. Push yourself to the limits that you think exist for you. Then watch as you go right through every single one of them. You will see that none exist.

Know You Will Have It

The easiest thing in the world for me is doing everything that I truly love to do. The hardest thing in the world for me is having the opportunity to do it all. But I will have it. You will too. Know that. The world is truly your oyster.

Honor the Quiet Moments

This has been a year full of quiet moments for me. I honor them. Sometimes, it is the quiet voice that keeps us going. It is the quiet voice that whispers, "don't give up yet" that keeps us getting back up. We are not always defined by our loudest moments, by our biggest moments. We are often defined by our quiet moments, the ones that no one else saw. When we had the strength to still listen to that quiet voice inside, to our belief, and we tried. Again. Honor these quiet moments in your life. Because in them, you get back up.

Thank Others

Sometimes I wonder if my parents would have preferred to have a different child. I know that they love me, with every fiber of their being, and would never trade me. I know this. But sometimes I wonder how they think about the role of being my mother and my father. I have never followed convention, I have rarely played by the rules, I have bucked the trends that people would have expected me to follow, and I have always, always, always thrown caution to the wind. I have jumped off cliffs, both figuratively and literally, and have rarely looked down to see what might be below me. I have just lived, without fear or concern, for what is expected of me and for the path that is right, safe or easier. I have not tried to make it harder on myself, or on them, truly. If a life that was more secure and more predictable made me happy, I honestly would have chosen it, because I want more than anything to feel secure. But security to me is not about money, or things, or anything outside of me. It is not about a job or a career or a house or a car. Even if a company could guarantee that I would never again have to worry about money, if my heart wasn't in it, I would never stay.

It is not easy to be a parent of a child who lives likes this, who believes this, who goes for it, each and every time, no matter what it costs. Every time, I choose to try, to believe, to dream, to reach and to stretch, even bigger. But when you live like this, you fall more than those who never risk anything. And my parents, each and every time, have always been there to offer a hand to help me back up. It isn't easy to spend 36 years doing this, and to never judge. I recognize this. It is not something that I take lightly. So I say to them, thank you. I am going for it right now in my life, more than I ever have. I am risking it all, to live the big dream and I will not take the easy path. I will not abandon my heart. It might cost me everything, but I have to do this.

So I honor my parents as incredible human beings, as beacons of light, of love and of belief. I know that this is hard on them and that it would be easier for them to sleep at night if I went and got a safer job, one that gave me financial security and a predictable path. They have opened their home to me, provided financial and emotional support in doing that, and have helped to give me the opportunity to launch this vision, to live my dream. And they have asked for nothing in return. Nothing. It takes an amazing parent to do this, unconditionally. I recognize them. For loving me as the woman that I want to become and for supporting me in the life that I want to lead. Not in what they want for me, but in what I want for me. I will not give up on this dream, on this vision that is unfolding before my very eyes. I can't. It's too important to me and is the piece that I have been seeking my whole life. It is here now, so I will walk forward into it and not look back. And as long as my heart is in it, I will stay. But this has been a hard journey on my parents. I know this. So Mom and Dad, thank you. I honor you, I celebrate you and I recognize the tremendous courage it has taken for you to keep believing in me, regardless of the life that I have chosen to lead. It hasn't been easy on you. But to me, it has been everything.

Thank the people that help you along the way. Thank the people that help you to fly.

Be in Awe

Today, I am in awe of my abilities, of my courage and of who I am. I walked through huge fears today. I was so uncomfortable doing it. I wanted to run. But I didn't. I stood in front of them, faced them down and walked through them. It isn't easy to do this. But it is intensely rewarding. When you do this, you get to experience yourself as the woman you are born to be. Free, unbridled, capable, unlimited. I am capable of anything. I now know this. It is what I wanted to know and now I do. I am in awe. Of me. Today, for a million and one reasons, stare in wonder and be in awe. Of you.

Support Each Other

To my friends, you are extraordinary. You have opened your hearts in a way that has given me the space in this world to learn, to connect, to feel, to express, to hurt, to heal, to release and to surrender, to everything. You have loved and supported me at every step of the way. You have walked with me as I have found my way. I would never be where I am without you. I know that. Today, I honor your hearts, your wisdom, your compassion, your spirit, your love and your support. As women, we must help each other. In this world, we can spend so much time tearing each other down, but we must stop. We must lift each other up. We must encourage and support each other along the way. We must be the wind at each other's backs. Because the only way that we will each get to our dreams is if we hold hands.

Admire Creation

Music is such an amazing part of my life. To those that create it, I admire your gifts. I would be lost without them. In all that you are willing to share in your music, and the courage that you show each time you honestly tell your stories and put your heart on the line, I feel what you feel. I feel your struggles, your pain, your triumphs and your journey. The emotions that we all feel are universal. So in all that you create, you connect us. In telling your story, you help us to feel. We need this. Please never stop sharing your brilliance. Your creations are a gift. They are treasured. Admire the creation that surrounds you, in whatever form it may be. It is what gives the world such beauty.

Go to These Places

I have dreamed of the places that I want to go to for so long, that I am afraid if I actually go to these places, I will no longer have my dream to look forward to. The dream of going to these places has motivated me for so much of my life and has driven me in everything I have done. But in this moment, I realize that I want to live my dream starting right now, not continue to live with my dream. So I will risk it. I will give up my dream of these places. And I will go. Whatever these places may be in your life, whatever the places are that you have dreamed about, go to them. Because once you are at these places, you will realize that they far outshine your dream.

Receive

I am learning to receive and am fighting not to give right back. Receiving for me is challenging because I am more comfortable giving. But if I never receive, then I will have nothing to give. I am experiencing this right now in my life. I have given so much. Yet I know that I cannot continue to give what I don't have. Something about my self-worth, something about believing that I am valuable and that the gifts that I am offering the world are valuable, is connected to my ability to receive. So I open my heart to the lesson. I open my heart to change. I will never succeed in the way that I want to without understanding, feeling and believing that I am worthy of receiving and that I must receive in order to live my best life. May I come to believe that what I have to offer the world is valuable and that I deserve to receive, everything that I am meant to receive. In your life, when someone gives something to you, learn to receive it. Own that you deserve to. Because you do. And remember, the experience of giving in this world can only exist for all of us if someone else is willing receive. So receive.

Connect to Your Fire

The fire within me must be reawakened. This journey has temporarily taken me away from the things that ignite it. For the time being, my body has given up a lot to follow my heart, to be away from the things that connect me to my fire, as I pursue what I want most and seek my greatest purpose in life. So I must relight the fire within me. I must connect to the things that make it burn. We each have different things in our lives that ignite our fire. You know what yours are. Connect to these things. Light the fire within you. And burn.

Build Your Empire

_____ *Single*

_____ *Taken*

__X__ *Building my empire*

I am. You should too. It is freedom.

Trust That All Roads Lead to Rome

All roads lead to Rome. These five legendary words are so simple and yet they say so much. I remembered them today and took them in as if my life depended on it, because in a way it does. I think that my greatest fear is that all of this work, all of this seeking, all of this journeying through the clutter and confusion and chaos will lead me to no other place than back to square one. A friend once said to me that you can't see how the dots are going to connect as you move forward through your life. It is only in looking backwards that you can see the line that connects them all, the line that is your life, and in doing this, you will see that the dots will all make sense. When you look backwards, it will be abundantly clear that every single dot, every step, had its purpose and was perfect, regardless of how wrong and confusing it may have felt at the time. Right now, it feels like the dots in my life are random and that I am being led down so many different roads. But I will trust that all of these dots have a purpose. And I will trust that all roads lead to Rome. To my perfect Rome, to the Rome that is waiting for me with open arms. Trust that you will always get to your Rome, even if the road that you're on right now doesn't seem to make sense. All of the roads in your life will lead you there.

Learn to Surrender

When I don't know something, I never want to surrender because surrendering seems so passive to me. It seems to be the weakest thing that I can do when I don't know something because I associate it with giving up control. But surrendering is actually acceptance. And once I surrender, once I accept that I don't know, the pressure to know then falls away. Then wisdom can arrive. Therefore, surrendering is the most powerful thing that I can do. I must learn to surrender. When you don't know something, surrender. You are not expected to know everything. Accept that you don't know. Because once you do, the answer will come in the moment that follows surrender. The wisdom that you are seeking will always arrive. There is such power in surrendering. So surrender, accept that you don't know. The moment you do, you will.

Be Willing to Not Know

There are goodbyes in my life right now, connected to things that I don't want to leave. But I know that I am meant to. I trust these goodbyes. In this moment, I can't see how these goodbyes are necessary for my best life or how they fit in to the bigger plan. But I will still say goodbye. I still trust that I am meant to. Living in this space after goodbye before the next beginning has arrived is hard. I don't know what will come next, but I am willing to sit in the space after these goodbyes. I am willing to not know. In your life, trust the goodbyes that you know you need to make and say them. Then be willing to sit in the space that follows them. Be willing to not know. Because miraculous beginnings are coming.

Breathe

Some days, it can feel like my life is moving so fast. And there is so much going on. And it is hard to keep up. And honestly, I forget to breathe. So I must stop. And breathe. It always brings me back to the present moment, and relaxes my mind. It slows down everything. So right now, just breathe. It simplifies everything. And remember, breathing is the only thing that you truly need to do to live.

Push Off from Small Shores

In the moments when I feel so unsure and am nostalgic for the predictable life that I've left, I always remind myself that the life that I am meant to live is so much bigger than that one that I have left behind. So I must keep pushing off from small shores. Today, I did again. And that means that I have now lost sight of the shore again which is a scary place to be. But my desire to reach my destiny is everything. So I have chosen to push off from this shore because I believe in the bigger shore that awaits, the shore that I cannot see. Yet. The shore that is waiting for you is so much more majestic than the one that you are leaving. Your destiny is so much bigger than the life that you are leaving behind. It is time to push off from the small shores in your life. Set sail.

Prove Them Wrong

There are people that tell me that this can't be done. There are people that tell me that there are too many obstacles in the way of making this entire vision that I now see for this mission a reality. To all of them, I say this: Do not tell me that it can't be done. I will do it. I will prove you wrong. Never let someone tell you that you can't do something. If they do, prove them wrong.

Follow Your Heart

Close Your Eyes.

Follow Your Heart.

I have. And I do.

I set out on this journey to find my greatest purpose. I committed to following my heart. The journey has led me to the truths that are in this book. They are the foundation upon which I now stand. At every turn, I have followed them. At every step, I have trusted them. You can too. They work. They will take you where you want to go. They have led me to my greatest purpose.

The Empowered Woman

This is my greatest purpose.

It is the vision that will transform the world by awakening every woman to her best self.

This book is just the beginning…

54533643R00069

Made in the USA
Columbia, SC
06 April 2019